NEVER TOO FAR GONE

A Study on the Book of Amos

This study belongs to:

_____

_____

KRYSTAL DICKSON

Never Too Far Gone: A Study on the Book of Amos
Copyright © 2025 by The Daily Grace Co.®
Spring, Texas. All rights reserved.

Unless otherwise noted, all Scripture quotations are taken from the Christian Standard Bible®, Copyright © 2020 by Holman Bible Publishers. Used by permission. Christian Standard Bible® and CSB® are federally registered trademarks of Holman Bible Publishers.

Scripture quotations marked (NLT) are taken from the Holy Bible, New Living Translation, copyright ©1996, 2004, 2015 by Tyndale House Foundation. Used by permission of Tyndale House Publishers, Carol Stream, Illinois 60188. All rights reserved.

The Daily Grace Co.® exists to equip disciples to know and love God and His Word by creating beautiful, theologically rich, and accessible resources so that God may be glorified and the gospel made known.

Designed in the United States of America and printed in China.

The message of Amos is as relevant today as it was thousands of years ago.

In This Study

INTRODUCTION	Before You Start

Study Suggestions 6

How to Study the Bible 8

The Attributes of God 10

Timeline of Scripture 12

Metanarrative of Scripture 14

Study Introduction 16

Bonus: Timeline of Events from Kingdom Split to Exile 18

Bonus: Outline of the Book of Amos 20

WEEK ONE	The Lord Roars from Zion

Week 1 Introduction + Memory Verse 22

Day 1: An Overview of Amos 25

Day 2: From Shepherd to Prophet 31

Day 3: God Reveals the Heart 37

Bonus: Oracles Against the Nations 43

Day 4: God Speaks to Judah and Israel 45

Day 5: The Sovereignty of a Holy God 51

WEEK TWO	Seek the Lord

Week 2 Introduction + Memory Verse 56

Day 1: The Point of No Return 59

Day 2: Seek the Lord and Live 65

Day 3: From Exodus to Exile 71

Day 4: Pride Comes Before the Fall 77

Day 5: The Unrelenting Lord 83

WEEK THREE	Hope for a Future

Week 3 Introduction + Memory Verse 88

Day 1: Feast to Famine 91

Day 2: The All-Knowing God of Armies 97

Day 3: Sifting of the Nations 103

Day 4: Hope is Here 109

Day 5: A Future Restored 115

What Is the Gospel? 120

Bibliography 123

Study Suggestions

We believe that the Bible is true, trustworthy, and timeless and that it is vitally important for all believers. These study suggestions are intended to help you more effectively study Scripture as you seek to know and love God through His Word.

SUGGESTED STUDY TOOLS

- [ ] Bible

- [ ] Double-spaced, printed copy of the Scripture passages that this study covers (You can use a website like www.biblegateway.com to copy the text of a passage and print out a double-spaced copy to be able to mark on easily.)

- [ ] Journal to write notes or prayers

- [ ] Pens, colored pencils, and highlighters

- [ ] Dictionary to look up unfamiliar words

HOW TO USE THIS STUDY

 ### Pray

Begin your study time in prayer. Ask God to reveal Himself to you, help you understand what you are reading, and transform you with His Word (Psalm 119:18).

 ### Read Scripture

Before you read what is written in each day of the study itself, read the assigned passages of Scripture for that day. Use your double-spaced copy to circle, underline, highlight, draw arrows, and mark in any way you would like to help you dig deeper as you work through a passage.

 ### Memorize Scripture

Each week of the study begins with a memory verse. You may want to write the verse down and put it in a place where you will see it often. We also recommend spending a few minutes memorizing the verse before you complete each day's study material.

 ### Read Study Content

Read the daily written content provided for the current study day.

 ### Respond

Answer the questions that appear at the end of each study day.

How to Study the Bible

*The inductive method provides tools for deeper and more intentional Bible study.
To study the Bible inductively, work through the steps below after
reading background information on the book.*

01 Observation & Comprehension
KEY QUESTION: WHAT DOES THE TEXT SAY?

After reading the daily Scripture in its entirety at least once, begin working with smaller portions of the Scripture. Read a passage of Scripture repetitively, and then mark the following items in the text:

- Key or repeated words and ideas
- Key themes
- Transition words (e.g., therefore, but, because, if/then, likewise, etc.)
- Lists
- Comparisons and contrasts
- Commands
- Unfamiliar words (look these up in a dictionary)
- Questions you have about the text

02 Interpretation
KEY QUESTION: WHAT DOES THE TEXT MEAN?

Once you have annotated the text, work through the following steps to help you interpret its meaning:

- Read the passage in other versions for a better understanding of the text.
- Read cross-references to help interpret Scripture with Scripture.
- Paraphrase or summarize the passage to check for understanding.
- Identify how the text reflects the metanarrative of Scripture, which is the story of creation, fall, redemption, and restoration.
- Read trustworthy commentaries if you need further insight into the meaning of the passage.

03 Application
KEY QUESTION: HOW SHOULD THE TRUTH OF THIS PASSAGE CHANGE ME?

Bible study is not merely an intellectual pursuit. The truths about God, ourselves, and the gospel that we discover in Scripture should produce transformation in our hearts and lives. Answer the following questions and prompts as you consider what you have learned in your study:

- What attributes of God's character are revealed in the passage?
- Consider places where the text directly states the character of God, as well as how His character is revealed through His words and actions.
- What do I learn about myself in light of who God is?
- Consider how you fall short of God's character, how the text reveals your sin nature, and what it says about your new identity in Christ.
- How should this truth change me?
- A passage of Scripture may contain direct commands telling us what to do or warnings about sins to avoid in order to help us grow in holiness. Other times, our application flows out of seeing ourselves in light of God's character. As we pray and reflect on how God is calling us to change in light of His Word, we should be asking questions like, "How should I pray for God to change my heart?" and "What practical steps can I take toward cultivating habits of holiness?"

The Attributes of God

Eternal
God has no beginning and no end. He always was, always is, and always will be.
HAB. 1:12 / REV. 1:8 / ISA. 41:4

Faithful
God is incapable of anything but fidelity. He is loyally devoted to His plan and purpose.
2 TIM. 2:13 / DEUT. 7:9 / HEB. 10:23

Good
God is pure; there is no defilement in Him. He is unable to sin, and all He does is good.
GEN. 1:31 / PS. 34:8 / PS. 107:1

Gracious
God is kind, giving us gifts and benefits we do not deserve.
2 KINGS 13:23 / PS. 145:8 ISA. 30:18

Holy
God is undefiled and unable to be in the presence of defilement. He is sacred and set-apart.
REV. 4:8 / LEV. 19:2 / HAB. 1:13

Incomprehensible
God is high above and beyond human understanding. He is unable to be fully known.
PS. 145:3 / ISA. 55:8-9 ROM. 11:33-36

Immutable
God does not change. He is the same yesterday, today, and tomorrow.
1 SAM. 15:29 / ROM. 11:29 JAMES 1:17

Infinite
God is limitless. He exhibits all of His attributes perfectly and boundlessly.
ROM. 11:33-36 / ISA. 40:28 PS. 147:5

Jealous
God is desirous of receiving the praise and affection He rightly deserves.
EXOD. 20:5 / DEUT. 4:23-24 JOSH. 24:19

Just
God governs in perfect justice. He acts in accordance with justice. In Him, there is no wrongdoing or dishonesty.
ISA. 61:8 / DEUT. 32:4 / PS. 146:7-9

Loving
God is eternally, enduringly, steadfastly loving and affectionate. He does not forsake or betray His covenant love.
JOHN 3:16 / EPH. 2:4-5 / 1 JOHN 4:16

Merciful
God is compassionate, withholding from us the wrath that we deserve.
TITUS 3:5 / PS. 25:10 LAM. 3:22-23

Omnipotent

God is all-powerful; His strength is unlimited.

MATT. 19:26 / JOB 42:1-2
JER. 32:27

Omnipresent

God is everywhere; His presence is near and permeating.

PROV. 15:3 / PS. 139:7-10
JER. 23:23-24

Omniscient

God is all-knowing; there is nothing unknown to Him.

PS. 147:4 / 1 JOHN 3:20
HEB. 4:13

Patient

God is long-suffering and enduring. He gives ample opportunity for people to turn toward Him.

ROM. 2:4 / 2 PET. 3:9 / PS. 86:15

Self-Existent

God was not created but exists by His power alone.

PS. 90:1-2 / JOHN 1:4 / JOHN 5:26

Self-Sufficient

God has no needs and depends on nothing, but everything depends on God.

ISA. 40:28-31 / ACTS 17:24-25
PHIL. 4:19

Sovereign

God governs over all things; He is in complete control.

COL. 1:17 / PS. 24:1-2
1 CHRON. 29:11-12

Truthful

God is our measurement of what is fact. By Him we are able to discern true and false.

JOHN 3:33 / ROM. 1:25 / JOHN 14:6

Wise

God is infinitely knowledgeable and is judicious with His knowledge.

ISA. 46:9-10 / ISA. 55:9 / PROV. 3:19

Wrathful

God stands in opposition to all that is evil. He enacts judgment according to His holiness, righteousness, and justice.

PS. 69:24 / JOHN 3:36 / ROM. 1:18

Timeline of Scripture

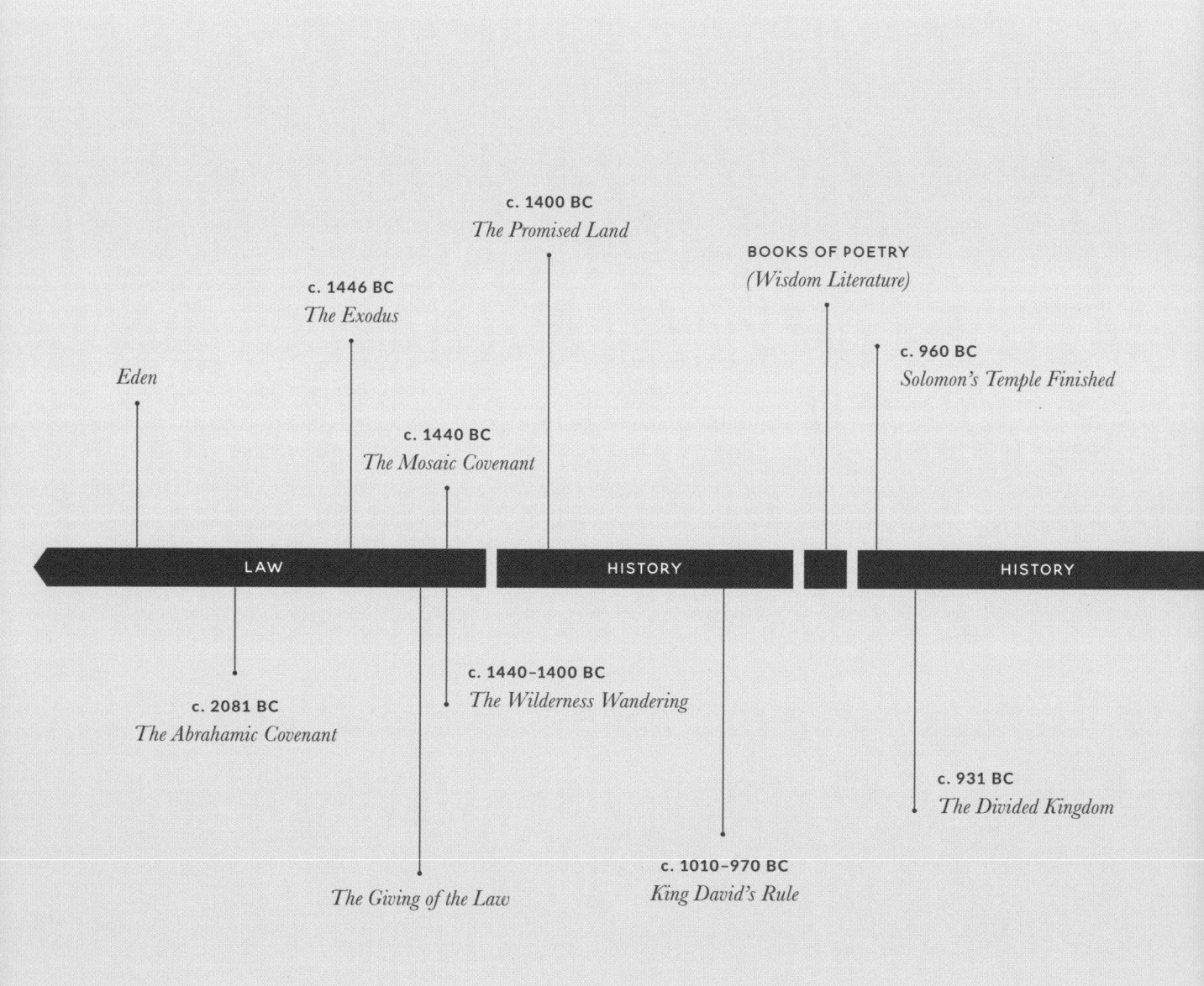

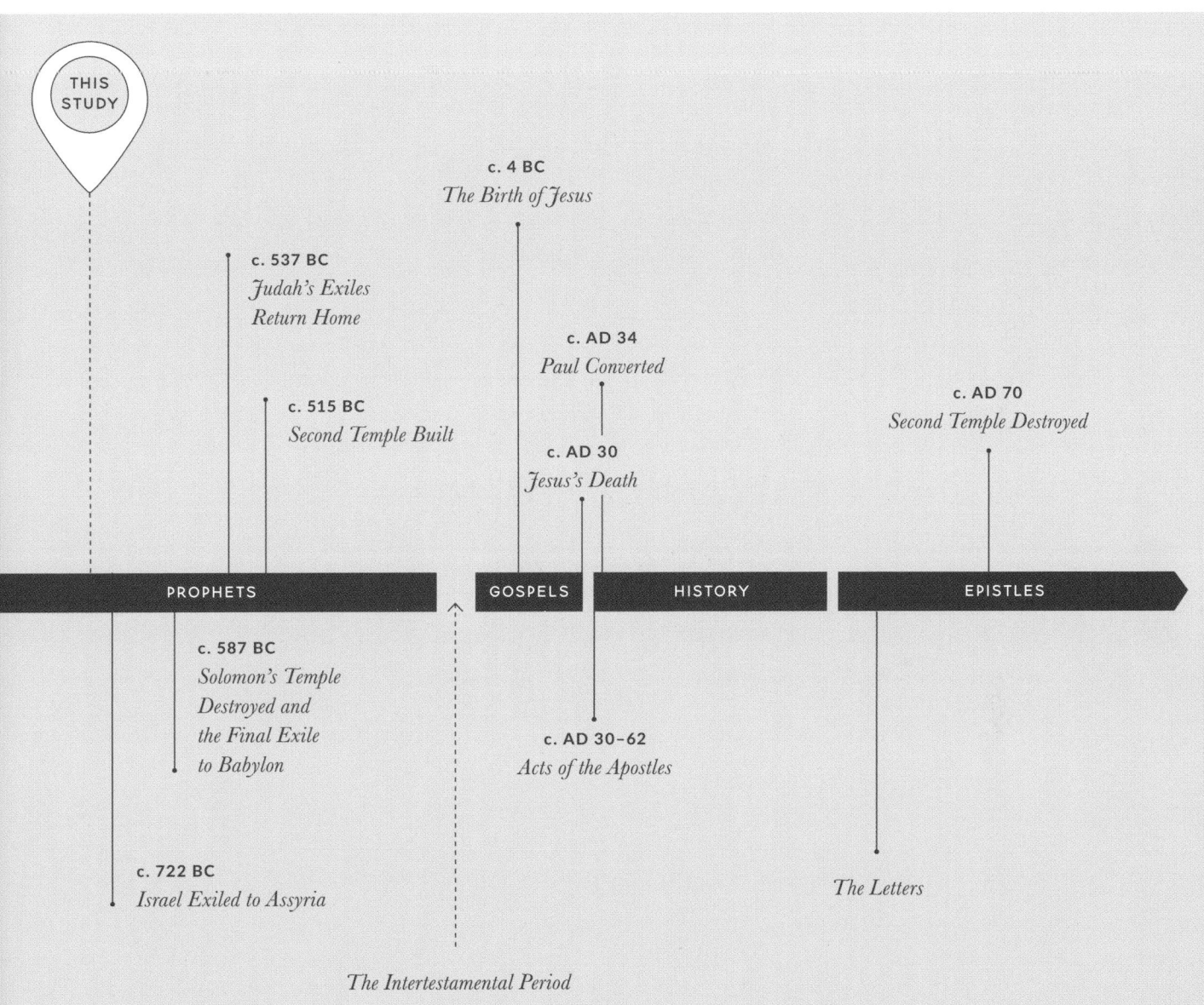

Timeline of Scripture

Metanarrative of Scripture

Creation

In the beginning, God created the universe. He made the world and everything in it. He created humans in His own image to be His representatives on the earth.

Fall

The first humans, Adam and Eve, disobeyed God by eating from the fruit of the Tree of Knowledge of Good and Evil. Their disobedience impacted the whole world. The punishment for sin is death, and because of Adam's original sin, all humans are sinful and condemned to death.

Redemption

God sent His Son to become a human and redeem His people. Jesus Christ lived a sinless life but died on the cross to pay the penalty for sin. He resurrected from the dead and ascended into heaven. All who put their faith in Jesus are saved from death and freely receive the gift of eternal life.

Restoration

One day, Jesus Christ will return again and restore all that sin destroyed. He will usher in a new heaven and new earth where all who trust in Him will live eternally with glorified bodies in the presence of God.

Study Introduction

Over the next three weeks, we will embark on a deep dive of a small yet neglected book of the Bible—the book of Amos. Perhaps it's a book you have read through quickly as a part of your yearly Bible reading plan. Maybe those pages in your Bible have remained untouched out of confusion. Without a guide, we can get lost in the maze of historical details and prophetic language. This study will be your guide as we marvel at the holiness of God, grieve over the sinfulness of humanity, and hope in the goodness of God through His Son, Jesus Christ.

Reading through the minor prophets can sometimes leave us with more questions than answers. So here are some tips as you read:

Consider the genre of Amos

Understanding the biblical genre of prophecy will help as you approach your study of Amos. Amos is considered to be a pre-exilic prophetic book, meaning Amos's prophecy came before God's people went into exile. Each prophet in the Old Testament received the Word of God and was tasked with sharing His message with a particular audience.

As God's messengers, the prophets exposed others' sin, announced God's judgment, called for repentance, and even proclaimed future restoration. Think of the prophets as alarm clocks, urgently calling God's people to "wake up" and repent of their sin—only for the people to continually hit the snooze button as they were lulled back to a destructive sleep.

The prophetic books are filled with dramatic imagery that communicates important truths about God. They often cover various time periods, as at times

they spoke about events that were about to happen and, at others, events that would not occur until much later. And sometimes they spoke about events that will not be fulfilled until Christ returns and establishes the glorious new heaven and new earth (Revelation 21:1–4).

Consider the value of reading Amos

When we approach the Bible, we are not seeking knowledge for the sake of knowledge. We are seeking God Himself as revealed in His Word. While we may be inclined to flip to more familiar books like Psalms or Philippians for our daily Bible reading, we know that all of Scripture is profitable (2 Timothy 3:16–17). From Genesis to Revelation, we get to see God's redemptive plan unfold as everything points to the person and work of Jesus Christ. Even in a short book like Amos, we can see Christ as our Redeemer, knowing that one day He will redeem all things.

Consider what God wants to show you while reading Amos

Don't gloss over the difficult sections, or genres, of Scripture. Instead, let it be an opportunity to depend fully on the Spirit. As you read, pray and ask the Holy Spirit to draw you close to Him. Pray that He would convict and guide you in your study. Deep study of God's Word will bear fruit in your life and will develop greater desire for God Himself. He is our greatest treasure.

Take your time as you read this prophetic book; ponder the imagery, learn from the judgments, consider the message God has for His people, and examine your own heart. Studying the prophets is a worthwhile exercise. May this time in the Word encourage your walk with the Lord and make you more like Him.

Timeline of Events from Kingdom Split to Exile

The book of Amos was written after the kingdom of Israel split into two separate kingdoms, with Israel to the north and Judah to the south, and before either kingdom was taken into exile. This timeline covers the history of the divided kingdom and the events of Amos prior to exile.

C. 931 BC

Unified Kingdom

- Solomon dies, and his son, Rehoboam, is named king of Israel (1 Kings 11:43).

- Northern tribes of Israel ask for less harsh conditions than what they endured under Solomon's leadership (1 Kings 12:4).

- Rehoboam refuses to alleviate their burden but rather intends to increase it (1 Kings 12:13–14).

The Divided Kingdom

- The northern tribes split from the southern tribes (1 Kings 12:15–24).

- The northern tribes of Israel make Jeroboam I their king (1 Kings 12:20).

- Jeroboam I creates an alternative religious system by establishing sanctuaries with golden calves in Bethel and Dan to prevent Israelites from going to Jerusalem and possibly staying in Judah permanently (1 Kings 12:25–30). Jeroboam I echoes the words spoken to Aaron, who, generations before, built a golden calf in the wilderness for the Israelites to worship (1 Kings 12:28, Exodus 32:4).

- The southern tribes, known as Judah, continue to be ruled by Rehoboam until Rehoboam dies, and his son takes his place as king (1 Kings 14:31).

C. 793 BC | C. 792/791 BC | C. 760 BC | C. 722 BC

Israel during the time of Amos | **Exile**

- Jeroboam II becomes king over Israel (2 Kings 14:23–24). He brings the nation into an era of prosperity and peace. This is the same Jeroboam mentioned in Amos 1:1.

- Uzziah, also known as Azariah, becomes king over Judah (2 Kings 15:1, Amos 1:1).

- Amos prophesies in Israel "two years before the earthquake" (Amos 1:1). Some scholars believe this is the same earthquake referenced in Zechariah 14:5.

- Just as God had warned Israel in Deuteronomy 28:64–68, the Assyrian Empire defeats the northern kingdom of Israel and carries much of its population into exile (2 Kings 17:6–23).

Outline of
the Book of Amos

Introduction .... Amos 1:1–2

ORACLES AGAINST THE NATIONS

Against Israel's Neighbors .... Amos 1:3–2:3

Against Judah .... Amos 2:4–5

Against Israel .... Amos 2:6–16

ORACLES OF JUDGMENT

Announcement Oracles .... Amos 3:1–5:17
("Listen to this message")

Woe Oracles .... Amos 5:18–6:14
("Woe to you/those")

VISIONS

Locusts .... Amos 7:1–3

Fire .... Amos 7:4–6

Plumb Line .... Amos 7:7–9

> Judgment Oracle Following Vision:
> *Amaziah the Priest in Bethel — Amos 7:10–17*

Fruit Basket .... Amos 8:1–3

> Judgment Oracle Following Vision:
> *Amos 8:4–14*

The Lord by the Altar .... Amos 9:1–10

ORACLES OF SALVATION

Restoration of the House of David .... Amos 9:11–12

Restoration of God's People and Land .... Amos 9:13–15

Week 1 Introduction

The Lord Roars from Zion

To start off this first week, you will read all nine chapters in the book of Amos, preferably in one sitting. This will greatly impact your overall understanding of the book. Keep in mind that this book contains a collection of oracles (messages from God), visions, and stories that encompass God's message to call His people to repentance and ultimately back to Himself. Amos often uses repetition and structure to communicate the themes in God's message, so reading the book in one sitting can help you to draw out those themes.

Set aside thirty minutes and read the book aloud, or read along while listening to an audio Bible. As you read through this book in its entirety, try not to get caught up in the details but look for the overall idea that God is communicating through Amos. Throughout this study, we will work through the text in smaller sections each day. Below is a highlighting guide to use as you study. As you read, consider using these highlighter colors to help you identify and remember key themes and ideas in the text.

Memory Verse

He is your praise and he is your God, who has done for you these great and awe-inspiring works your eyes have seen.

Deuteronomy 10:21

The judgment of God is meant to soften hard hearts and lead His people back to Himself.

Week 1 Day 1

An Overview of Amos

> Practice This Week's Memory Verse

> Read Amos 1:1–9:15

In the eighth century BC, God called an ordinary shepherd from Judah to proclaim His message to Israel, the chosen but rebellious people of God. Like other prophets, Amos's message was one of judgment over sin committed against a holy God and His people. At the heart of this book, we see God's faithfulness in light of Israel's hard-hearted unfaithfulness. God was faithful to Israel as they fled from Egypt. God was faithful to Israel in the wilderness. God was faithful as they entered the Promised Land. Every step of the way, God remained faithful to His people.

During the reign of Jeroboam II, the northern kingdom of Israel was experiencing an era of prosperity and political stability unlike anything it had seen since it split from the southern kingdom of Judah in c. 931 BC. The Israelites practiced outward expressions of religiosity while also accumulating excessive wealth and oppressing the poor. Even so, Israel interpreted the peace and prosperity they were experiencing as a sign that God was indeed pleased with them. After all, they were His chosen people. The people of Israel assumed that since God made a covenant with them, this would be enough to shield them from the consequences of their sin.

Enter Amos, a shepherd who is given the unpleasant task of telling Israel that the opposite was true: God's judgment is upon *all* who turn away from Him, including Israel. God had delivered them from oppression in Egypt only to see His people step into the role of the oppressor, and He makes it clear that their sins deserve His wrath. Not only will God hold them accountable, but as Amos will point out several times, God will bring their nation to an end. God will send them into exile because of their habitual unfaithfulness, just as He had warned them through Moses (Deuteronomy 28:15, 64–68). No number of armies or amount of material wealth can protect Israel from the utter destruction that will be laid upon them.

As we venture through these nine short chapters together, we will see how Amos continually points us back to God and His plan of redemption. The judgment of God is meant to soften hard hearts and lead His people back to Himself. With all the dark imagery and intense language that accompanies God's judgment, we run the risk of missing the beauty of God as He demands justice for those who endure unrelenting mistreatment. Amos will show how deeply God cares about how His image-bearers are treated.

Reading the prophets can feel like learning a foreign language. It can be tempting to quickly gloss over places we do not know, names we cannot pronounce, and ancient rituals that are unfamiliar to us—all blanketed by the dark, heavy cloud of God's anger and judgment. It is no wonder why the prophets often get neglected in our Bible reading! Their message can feel lost in time, without any real implications for us as modern-day readers.

However, the message of Amos is as relevant today as it was thousands of years ago. Injustice and abuse of power still plague our world today. We see evidence of this brokenness regularly on the news. We experience it in our own lives. We cannot escape it, even as we scroll through social media. The effects of sin are evident as we witness how God's image-bearers are mistreated or are mistreating others. It is easy to see why this would be a message we need today.

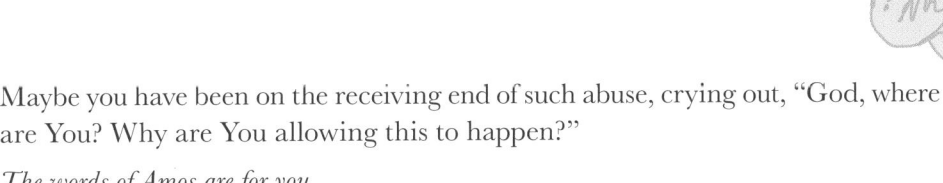

Maybe you have been on the receiving end of such abuse, crying out, "God, where are You? Why are You allowing this to happen?"

The words of Amos are for you.

Perhaps you are walking in shame over your own failings in how you treat others, wondering, "God, am I too far gone to receive Your mercy?"

The words of Amos are for you.

There is hope found in the pages of Amos. He concludes the book by describing a future day when God will restore what is broken, a day when Israel's inheritance will be secured once again. Likewise, our hope lies in the restoration that is ultimately found through the life, death, and resurrection of Jesus Christ, and one day He will come again to restore creation—to make all things new.

"But let justice flow like water, and righteousness, like an unfailing stream" (Amos 5:24). These are the very words of God spoken through His servant, Amos. This is not a book lost in time—it is a book for us today.

> Amos will show how deeply God cares about how His image-bearers are treated.

reflect

How would you describe the main idea of Amos?
What words or phrases are repeated throughout the book?

What aspects of God's character did you see as you read?
Review the attributes of God on pages 10–11.

What do you hope to gain from this study?

notes

He is the God who speaks,
and He has chosen Amos to be His mouthpiece.

Week 1 Day 2

From Shepherd to Prophet

> Practice This Week's Memory Verse

> Read Amos 1:1–2, 7:14–15; Deuteronomy 18:18–22

The role of a prophet was a difficult one. As the bearer of God's bad news, Amos had the task of preaching a message that no one wanted to hear. Not only would Amos expose Israel's actions as wicked and deserving of punishment, but he would point to the fact that their empty religious practices were just as sinful. Amos declared that Israel's affiliation as God's chosen people would not be enough to save them from God's judgment. Why would Amos leave everything behind to preach to a nation that seems to think they are exempt from the very message God has for them? These first two verses in Amos provide us with the historical context to set the stage for what God intends to accomplish through this unlikely prophet.

By citing the reigns of two kings, Uzziah in Judah (who is also known as Azariah) and Jeroboam II in Israel, we can place Amos's ministry during the time of 2 Kings 14:23–15:7. While Amos went to the northern kingdom of Israel during his prophetic ministry, it was the southern kingdom of Judah that received the recorded account of this book many years later. They likely recognized the authenticity of Amos's prophecy since Israel's destruction had already come to pass by this point. This brief introduction confirms that both the messenger and the message are to be trusted. For the audience, then and now, Israel's unfaithfulness and ultimate demise is a cautionary tale.

Consider how the message of Amos begins in verse 2: "The Lord roars from Zion and makes his voice heard from Jerusalem." The imagery used here is vivid, and it commands our attention. Roaring evokes urgency, not complacency or apathy. Clearly, the one true God has something important to say and demands that His voice be heard. He is the God who speaks, and He has chosen Amos to be His mouthpiece. God Himself is at the center of the message Amos brings to Israel, a nation that has refused to live in a way that honors Him. He is the God who speaks. But will Israel listen?

The fact that Jerusalem is mentioned here shows that God is not identifying with the northern kingdom of Israel at this moment but with the southern kingdom of Judah. We know from Amos 7:10–13 that Amos spent some time prophesying in Bethel, a city in the southern part of Israel. Rather than being a "house of God," as the meaning of the city's name suggests, Bethel had become a breeding ground of syncretism. Syncretism means that the worship of various other gods was taking place alongside the worship of God. Even so, God makes it clear that He is sovereign and Lord over all of creation. The theme of God's authority over all creation will develop throughout the book. All things are subject to God's authority, and His voice has the power to bring life or cause destruction.

Outside of this introduction and his brief encounter with Amaziah in chapter 7, not much else is revealed about the prophet Amos. What we do know is that God chose him to speak to the stubborn, hard hearts of His people. Amos obeyed in faith because he recognized that God called him to be a prophet, and it was God's message he was presenting. God had something important to say to His people, and He chose Amos to be His voice. Amos was not chosen because he had a well-known reputation for public speaking. By his own admission, he was not equipped to be a prophet (Amos 7:14–15). God could have easily orchestrated a different set of circumstances for Amos to fulfill this mission. He could have made Amos the son of a prophet or given him the experience needed to prepare him for this task. God could have chosen to use a different prophet altogether.

But in His wisdom, God chose an ordinary person to preach His extraordinary message. Amos had the one thing he needed to fulfill this calling on his life—God Himself. God called Amos to go, so Amos went.

Israel neglected to worship God and refused to listen to His voice. Now it was Amos's duty to lay out the impending judgment Israel deserved for its wickedness. God spoke powerfully through Amos, a shepherd He called to expose the ways Israel had failed to uphold the Law. God speaks through His Word today too, and by it, we are exposed to our own wickedness. We cannot uphold the Law by our works, no matter how good we try to be. But God provided a way for us through Jesus Christ, our Good Shepherd, who perfectly fulfilled the Law that we failed to obey. If we are in Christ, we are freed from the penalty of our sin, knowing that Christ fully paid it when He went to the cross. When sheep hear the voice of their loving yet firm shepherd, they follow after it (John 10:4). We can hear our Good Shepherd's voice as we seek Him in His Word. He is still the God who speaks to us today.

> All things are subject to God's authority, and His voice has the power to bring life or cause destruction.

reflect

What is the role of a prophet (Deuteronomy 18:18–22)?
How do you see this reflected in Amos?

How does Amos's journey from shepherd to prophet
encourage you in your own faith journey?

In what ways does God's Word expose your need for Jesus?
Write a prayer thanking God that He provided a way for
redemption through Jesus's life, death, and resurrection.

notes

How we treat others will reveal our hearts
and what we ultimately worship.

Week 1 Day 3

God Reveals the Heart

> Practice This Week's Memory Verse

> Read Amos 1:3–2:3, Romans 2:14–16

The foreign nations surrounding Israel are under examination as Amos proclaims God's judgment over each of them. All nations have exceeded God's patience with their sins against humanity, and He will judge accordingly. Though the circumstances vary from nation to nation, they are each guilty of the same crime—mistreating people made in the image of God. We learn a lot about the nature of God when we see what makes Him angry. God's image-bearers are being treated as objects, and His response to the nations shows that He always stands with the oppressed.

Amos employs the same repetitive structure as he confronts each nation. Each oracle opens with God refusing to relent "for three crimes, even four" (Amos 1:3, 1:6, 1:9, 1:11, 1:13, 2:1). Rather than take this as a literal statement, we are meant to understand that God refuses to be silent amid ongoing oppression. He can no longer withhold punishment from these nations. Amos describes the central reason for each nation's judgment and declares God's punishment accordingly.

Amos first presents God's case against Damascus, which is located in Aram, also known as Syria. Amos calls out the heinous abuse of the Syrians by using the imagery of threshing, which involved dragging a board with sharp nails over grain and ripping it from its stalk. This paints a vivid picture of the gruesome treatment of others at the hands of Syrians. God makes it clear that He is more powerful than the greatest of their political and military strongholds. From the Valley of Aven to Beth-eden, God's judgment will leave nothing untouched—it will be a complete conquest (Amos 1:5). Everything they had worked for will be gone (2 Kings 16:9, Isaiah 17:1).

Next, Amos turns his attention to the Philistines in Gaza. The Philistines took an entire population of people and sold them into slavery. The people's value was determined by the highest bidder, seen here as the Edomites, and the people were stripped of their human dignity and rights. God demands death for those who commit such a horrific crime (Exodus 21:16). Thus Amos prophesies that the Philistines will perish (2 Kings 18:8).

The next two oracles are against Tyre and Edom. Tyre was a prosperous city and a significant trading hub. Because of Tyre's location on the coast, they would pack their ships full of captives and send them off into a life of slavery. The oracle against Edom condemns unprovoked and ongoing violence toward others. These two cities are connected through "brotherhood" and "brother" language, as Tyre broke a peace treaty with nations by selling slaves from their communities (Amos 1:9), and Edom acted upon deep-seated hatred toward his brother (Amos 1:11), possibly against neighboring Judah. As Israel heard of God's judgment upon Edom, it may have hit a little closer to home for them. Amos started with the foreign nations but is now condemning their distant relatives (Genesis 36:1). It would not take long before the spotlight would shine the brightest on them.

The last two oracles are against Ammon and Moab. The Ammonites are condemned for attacking the vulnerable, even inflicting violence against pregnant women. They committed genocide to wipe out the existing and future population—all for accumulating more land. Personal greed and ambition outweighed any regard for the helpless, and as a result, the Ammonite leaders would be taken into exile. God condemns Moab for burning the bones of the king of Edom. Many scholars see this to be an intentional act of vengeance against the deceased, for burning the bones was meant to prevent their future participation in the resurrection. Both the Ammonites and Moabites had no regard for human life as they actively destroyed any hope for their future.

Though these are Gentile nations that do not have a covenant relationship with God, they are still under judgment. They are not exempt from obeying their moral conscience (Romans 2:14–15). Amos concludes this oracle, like many others previously, with "The Lord has spoken" (Amos 2:3). These words come from God, revealing His omniscience as He provides great detail over the nations' past and present sins. They should receive these words with great fear and reverence for Yahweh—the one true God.

How we treat others will reveal our hearts and what we ultimately worship. We may treat this as two different commands to obey—treat people made in God's image with dignity and worship the one true God. However, these commands are inextricably intertwined. Jesus tells us that we are to love God with all our hearts, souls, minds, and strength and to love our neighbors as ourselves (Mark 12:29–31). By loving God and loving our neighbors, we align our hearts to His, and the world will see that we belong to Him alone. We should care a great deal about the things—and the people—that God cares about.

Like these nations, our sin is not hidden from God. Our entire lives have been laid bare before Him. When confronted with our own sinfulness, we are also presented with a choice. Will we choose to go deeper in our sin, or will we turn and gaze upon Jesus? God's kindness is meant to lead us to repentance (Romans 2:4), so we can turn from our rebellious ways and worship Him alone. Repentance allows us to live our lives anew, being washed by the blood of Christ and cleansed of our sins. When we fail to obey, we do not have to sit in the shame of our sin. Instead, we can turn to God and rejoice in the freedom that only Christ can bring. He remembers your sins no more.

reflect

What did these nations seem to value most? Where do you see yourself placing value on things apart from Christ?

Read Psalm 103:6–14. How can God's care for the oppressed bring comfort in times of suffering?

Are there sins that you have been minimizing or trying to hide from God? Spend some time with God, confessing your sin honestly and specifically. Conclude your time by praising God for His unending mercy.

notes

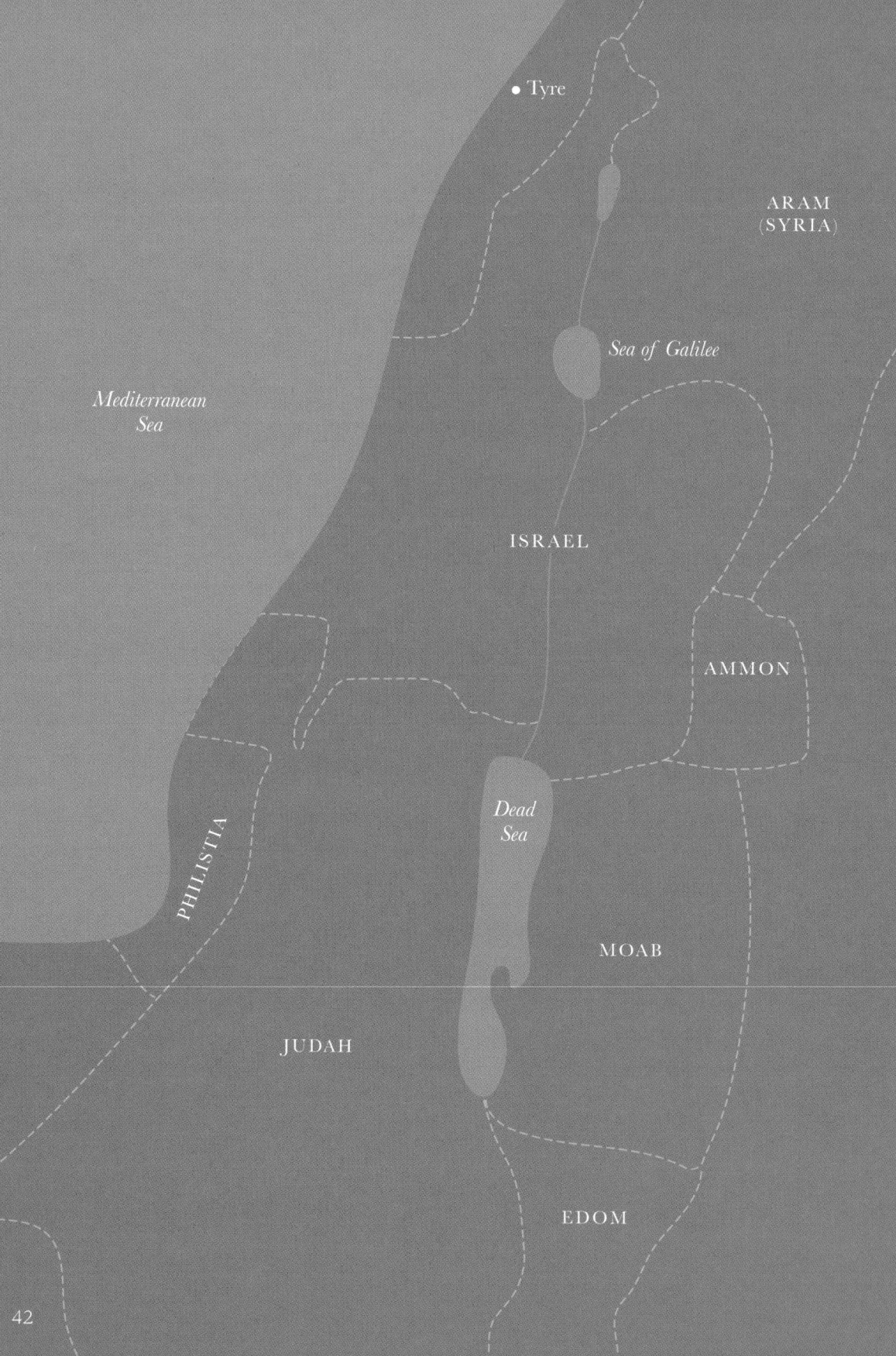

Oracles Against the Nations

In the first two chapters of his prophetic book, the prophet Amos declares God's judgment against Israel, Judah, and the surrounding nations. This includes Aram*, Philistia, Tyre, Edom, Ammon, and Moab. The map on the left shows the location of each of these nations in relation to Israel and Judah.

Editors' Note: Some Bible translations translate the nation of "Aram" as "Syria," while others translate it as "Aram." However, both of these names refer to the same kingdom and nation.

- Aram — *Amos 1:3–5*
- Philistia — *Amos 1:6–8*
- Tyre — *Amos 1:9–10*
- Edom — *Amos 1:11–12*
- Ammon — *Amos 1:13–15*
- Moab — *Amos 2:1–3*
- Judah — *Amos 2:4–5*
- Israel — *Amos 2:6–16*

Throughout the Bible, God calls His people
to remember who He is
and what He has done for them.

Week 1 Day 4

God Speaks to Judah and Israel

> Practice This Week's Memory Verse

> Read Amos 2:4–16, Romans 2:17–24

Israel's prideful gaze was upon everyone but themselves. They basked in the glow of God's holy anger unleashed on the surrounding nations. There was no love lost between Israel and these neighbors. The people of Israel had what the others did not have—an identity as God's elect, His chosen people. But if you were to draw a line connecting the nations in the order of Amos's oracles against them, that line would criss-cross over the entire region, with Israel right in the center. Because of the order in which Amos addresses each nation, this encircling pattern is often referred to by scholars as the noose tightening around Israel's neck. It appears that Israel was the intended target of God's most severe indictment.

Though Amos's tone and structure are patterned similarly to his previous oracles, the reasons for God's judgment against Judah and Israel differ drastically. The gaze of Israel shifts from their neighbors and happily lands on their rival as Amos addresses the sin of Judah. It is interesting to note that Judah is not charged with the mistreatment of others but rather with listening to man's words over God. They had direct access to the God who speaks, yet they chose to ignore His voice. If the other nations are subject to their own God-given consciences regarding moral living (Romans 2:14–16), then Judah is condemned for failing to uphold God's law (Romans 2:17–24).

Reluctantly, Israel's gaze must now turn inward as God's anger is on display toward them. Israel earns the longest and most critical of Amos's oracles. Instead of highlighting one sin, Amos lists many sins that Israel is guilty of committing, which makes them sound a lot like their pagan neighbors. Amos will spend the rest of the book describing how Israel has been unfaithful to their God who has remained faithful to them. Israel cheapened God's grace and abused His patience toward them in their disobedience. This bolsters the severity of God's wrath, as they had the means and opportunity to turn their hearts back to God, yet they failed to do so. Their role as God's elect gives way to their unique punishment. God continually reminds Israel of their covenantal relationship and thus the basis for the judgment leveled against them. Any perception of favoritism they thought they had was gone.

In chapter 2, Amos provides a stark contrast between who Israel had been and who they had become. Verses 6–8 depict Israel as the oppressor, sinning against God and His people with callous intentionality. The wealthy would abuse the poor over something trivial like a pair of sandals, and the powerful committed sexual sin that rivaled the pagans and defied God's law against such misconduct (Leviticus 18:6–18). The self-righteous abused God's law by keeping the garments of those who owed money (Exodus 22:25–27) and taking wine as payment. The garments were brought to the sanctuary as a badge of honor, and wine was consumed as a drink offering. Evidence of their unrepentant sin against a holy God accompanied them to His altar.

Yet verses 9–12 call back to the former years of Israel as the oppressed and God as their deliverer. God calls them again to remember His presence and provision, as well as their true identity as a wholly dependent people. God was faithful to lead them out of Egypt. He was faithful to be with them in the wilderness. He provided leaders and prophets so that they would continue seeking holiness and righteous living. Israel had seen the Lord do great and awe-inspiring works on their behalf (Deuteronomy 10:21). And yet, they continued to reject God's provision.

And so Amos concludes with a grim look into Israel's future. Their security in their national identity, military stability, and excess wealth cannot and will not save them from the wrath that is coming.

This message casts a dark shadow over everything. In Israel's golden age of prosperity, these are probably the last things they would expect to happen. While the other nations would still be accountable for their wicked behavior, God would treat His chosen people, the ones who knew Him and His law, with even more severity. Israel was to reflect the goodness of God in the way they lived. God Himself was the model for His people. His care for Israel was to be the blueprint for them to follow. They were to love others as He loved them. There was a division between Judah and Israel, but they were both recipients of God's mercy when He brought them out of Egypt. Yet, the judgment oracles of these first two chapters conclude not in victory but in defeat for Israel. Israel was likely waiting for Amos to share how God would act on their behalf and conquer their enemies. Instead, they were left with the weightiness of their sin and questions left unanswered. Where was God's goodness now? Will God remain faithful to His promises?

Throughout the Bible, God calls His people to remember who He is and what He has done for them. Amos calls the Israelites to remember while also revealing the deserved condemnation for their self-serving ways. We experience a similar tension as we seek to know God more. He is a merciful God, but we know that He is also just. Though the punishment for our sin is death, we have been freely justified through Christ, our Redeemer (Romans 3:23–24). The price for our sin has been fully paid through His shed blood on the cross—what a joyous truth to remember today.

reflect

How often do you reflect on God's goodness?
Spend some time listing the ways He is good to you.

When are you tempted to compare yourself to someone else?
What is the standard of holiness?

Summarize these first two chapters of Amos by filling out this chart.
How is each group guilty of rejecting God and His commands?
What similarities or differences do you see in each group?

Israel's neighbors (Amos 1:3–2:3)	Judah (Amos 2:4–5)	Israel (Amos 2:6–16)

notes

God is the divine author of history, sovereign over times of prosperity and times of utter devastation.

Week 1 Day 5

The Sovereignty of a Holy God

> Practice This Week's Memory Verse

> Read Amos 3:1–15

The book of Amos opens with the Lord roaring with urgency (Amos 1:2), and Amos continues to magnify His voice through a new set of three oracles directed at Israel. Known as the announcement oracles (Amos 3:1–5:17), the structure and aim of these differ from the previous oracles. Each begins with the plea for the audience to "listen to this message" (Amos 3:1) as they have yet to listen to God's voice thus far. Through these three oracles, Amos will plead God's case that Israel's judgment is deserved and necessary. Amos acknowledges that Israel does have a special identity as the people of God. The Israelites were known personally by God Himself, which set them apart from everyone else. They also experienced God's faithfulness as He brought them out of Egypt and into the Promised Land. But to Israel's dismay, Amos points to their identity as the basis for God's judgment.

As a shepherd from Judah, Amos was likely criticized for coming against Israel with such boldness—and on their own turf, no less. Did Israel really deserve the full wrath of God? Does the punishment fit the crime? After all, they were performing their religious practices by visiting the temple and giving sacrifices as commanded in the Law (Amos 4:4–5, 5:4–6). Their covenant with God came with privileges, but it also came with the responsibility to obey Him. The providential care of God throughout their history should have caused them to stand in awe before Him. Instead, they attempted to hide behind the covenant to protect themselves from the consequences of their wicked actions.

Through a series of rhetorical questions, Amos argues why he must preach this particular message to this particular group. There is a distinct pattern throughout verses 3–8 to prove there is a reason behind everything that happens to them. God wants to ensure through plain language that the Israelites understand. These questions argue that Israel should not be surprised by the consequences of their actions, nor should they dismiss God at work, even in the midst of destruction. God is the divine author of history, sovereign over times of prosperity and times of utter devastation. Not a single thing happens apart from the perfect wisdom of God. If God can bring destruction to the nations, He can bring destruction to His wayward people. In light of all this, how could Amos do anything but prophesy and speak on behalf of the Lord over all creation?

Israel's capital city of Samaria is in full view as Amos invites the Philistines (of Ashdod) and the Egyptians to look upon Israel's oppression of the vulnerable and poor (Amos 3:9). Even the pagans can attest to the deserved punishment of Israel's actions. There is no partiality when it comes to God's justice. The wealthy residents of Samaria are "incapable of doing right" (Amos 3:10). Samaria is situated safely in the mountains, supposedly protected from their enemies as they promote and celebrate such evil deeds.

In His perfect wisdom, the sovereign God chooses to use Israel's enemies as the means of His judgment (Amos 3:11) to attack Samaria, which Israel believed to be secure. What a shock that must have been to the Israelites! Though Amos does not explicitly mention this, we know that God used the Assyrian empire to ultimately accomplish His purposes (2 Kings 17:21–24). In Israel's time of prosperity and peace, Assyria had been quietly lurking in the background and would go on to force Israel into exile around 722 BC—within a single generation of Amos's audience.

But Amos's message is not all doom and gloom. Chapter 3 provides us with our first glimmer of hope for a redemptive future for Israel. Amos's vivid description suggests that redemption will still be possible. Still, only a small remnant will be ripped from the lion's mouth as the nation of Israel is destroyed. The number will be small in comparison to the widespread destruction. This brief interjection shows us that God still sees something worth saving in His people. However, the emphasis of this chapter remains on the judgment that Israel has brought upon themselves, as Amos concludes this oracle with a glimpse into Israel's future punishment. Notice the language used to describe how God will demolish, destroy, and bring Israel's luxuries to an end (Amos 3:15). The creator God, who upholds the entire universe, will employ His full power to bring Israel to the end of themselves.

The Lion roars before He pounces as a warning that He is about to take action. God's elect will be led into exile. All hope and security they found in maintaining peace and prosperity will be destroyed. In God's Word, we can heed the warnings of those who decide to go their own way and abandon the commands of Scripture. God has given us all we need in life and enables us through the Holy Spirit to live a life of godliness (2 Peter 1:3). We also see the blessings of a life devoted to God, His Word, and His glory. God disciplines those He loves, and though it is painful, it yields for us the fruit of righteousness (Hebrews 12:5–11). God uses circumstances, even disaster, to accomplish His purpose in our lives. Hundreds of years after Amos's prophecy, God would ultimately accomplish His redemptive work by sacrificing His one and only Son, Jesus Christ, the Lion of Judah (Revelation 5:5). Because of the grace we have been given through Christ, we can honestly face our sin and suffering before God. Our hope and our security are found in God alone.

reflect

Where are you tempted to find your security other than Christ?

How has God used difficult circumstances,
even disaster, to draw you closer to Him?

How does God's sovereignty help you navigate painful seasons in life?

notes

Week 2 Introduction

Seek the Lord

This week, we will cover Amos 4–7. Though these chapters are short, they cover quite a bit of ground.

Keep in mind the historical context of Amos's prophetic ministry. The harsh judgments and sorrowful laments were in stark contrast to Israel's comfortable and lavish lifestyles. They were living in a state of political peace and material prosperity, blind to their own idolatry and sin. Like Israel, we often lack the perspective needed to see our sin clearly. Our actions have eternal implications—for better or worse. Israel couldn't see that their atrocious behavior was first and foremost sin against a holy and righteous God. They diminished the dignity of others made in God's image. And so Amos will remind Israel once again that their actions have dire consequences.

Before you start this week's content, spend time reviewing the previous week's chapters and memory verse. Pray that the Lord would help you to delight in Him as you study His Word. Ask God to protect your heart against lesser loves competing for your affections. Use the space below to write out a simple prayer before starting week two's content.

Memory Verse

But let justice flow like water, and righteousness, like an unfailing stream.

Amos 5:24

In His patience and with great restraint,
God moved toward His people

Week 2 Day 1

The Point of No Return

> Practice This Week's Memory Verse

> Read Amos 4:1–13

Over the generations, a chasm had slowly started to form. On one side, a just and holy God beckoned for Israel to return to Him. He remained steadfast, ever faithful to His people, and jealous for their worship. Far on the other side of the chasm stood His wayward people, comfortable with their sin and their superficial religion. God wanted wholehearted devotion from His people. They wanted an easy life and a comfortable imitation of faith.

Amos further condemns Samaria's lavish and oppressive lifestyle as he confronts the "cows of Bashan." Initially, this might sound like a general derogatory name used for women, but it is helpful to know why God mentions Bashan in the first place. This district was known for large, well-fed cattle and rich, fertile land. This imagery shows that Amos is disparaging the wealthy women who habitually chose to overindulge, like the fattened cows in Bashan, while trampling on the weak and vulnerable. Amos declares that his next words are those that "the Lord God has sworn by his holiness" (Amos 4:2). An oath made by God is as good as God Himself. The trustworthiness of His words is evidenced by God's very existence. Swearing by His holiness confirms the punishment He sees fit for a people who seek personal fulfillment over personal holiness—being taken away with fishhooks and driven out of the city.

There is debate on the Hebrew translation of "hooks" and if this description is meant to be figurative or literal. There is evidence that suggests that Assyrian soldiers placed hooks through the jaws or noses of their captives. Then, they would attach ropes to the hooks and use those ropes to transport their prisoners. Amos could also be alluding to a fisherman who would drag fish on the same hooks he used to catch them. Regardless of the interpretation, the description is gruesome, pointing to a devastating conclusion to their story. The mention of breaches in the wall in Amos 4:3 looks into the future in which some significant event, such as an earthquake or war, will cause large holes and cracks in the protective walls surrounding Samaria. Those who survive will be stripped from the comforts of luxury, dragged out of the city, and plunged into the darkness of exile.

Amos then exposes the irony and blatant hypocrisy of Israel's religious rituals (Amos 4:4–5). Their sacrifices and tithes were frequent, and they performed voluntary offerings that God had not commanded of them. They also ensured that their good works were heard by all who were around them. However, even through all of the offerings and sacrifices, they still neglected the basic tenets of their faith to love God and keep His commands. Israel had perfected the outward appearance of going through the motions and doing the "right things" yet having an apathetic, distant heart toward God.

In His patience and with great restraint, God moved toward His people as He orchestrated trials, plagues, and hardships that were meant to draw Israel back to Himself (Amos 4:6–11). However, in their rebellion, God's people continually move away from Him. The chasm deepened and widened with each instance of complacency and every self-serving act. Even in the face of outright defiance, God's love for His people still abounds. They habitually abuse the mercy of God. God's lament over Israel culminates in the repeated refrain with each divine intervention, "yet you did not return to me" (Amos 4:11). Instead, Israel

refuses to listen to God, thus taking on the character of their former oppressor, Pharaoh (Exodus 8:32).

As a result, Amos concludes chapter 4 with a promise that they will meet their God! Previously, this would have led the Israelites to rejoice, but now, as they sit in their sin, this should only produce fear at the thought of facing a holy God. The last verse in this chapter is a hymn or "doxology," which is "an ascription of praise or glory to God in song or prayer . . ." (Douglas and Tenney, 371). It proclaims God's power and authority over all creation. But Israel was still unwilling to change their ways. In 1 Timothy 6:17–19, Paul warns Timothy of the same concerns; it seems the early church wrestled with the same issues that were present in ancient Israel:

> Instruct those who are rich in the present age not to be arrogant or to set their hope on the uncertainty of wealth, but on God, who richly provides us with all things to enjoy. Instruct them to do what is good, to be rich in good works, to be generous and willing to share, storing up treasure for themselves as a good foundation for the coming age, so that they may take hold of what is truly life.

Like Paul calls Timothy, so Amos calls God's people to holy living—a call to listen to and obey the Lord. This is a command to put away self-serving desires and worship God over material things. This is a plea to reject empty religious practices in favor of a holy, God-honoring life that flows from a changed heart. The same call to holiness from thousands of years ago is before us today. The widening chasm between Israel and their God seemed impossible to cross without divine intervention—an act of God. For us today, we can look to the old rugged cross, stained by the precious blood of our Savior, as a reminder that the distance between God and us is no more. He brought us from darkness to light (1 Peter 2:9). Dark emptiness has been filled with the light of the glory of God (2 Corinthians 4:6). It is only by God's great mercy that sinful people can be brought into His presence. Now, nothing can separate us from His love (Romans 8:38–39).

reflect

Read Deuteronomy 28:15–26. How does this passage impact how you read Amos? What connections do you see between these curses and the events listed in Amos 4:6–11?

Consider the outward expressions of your faith. In what ways are you tempted to "go through the motions" or think your standing before God is based on your good works?

What role do money or possessions have in your life? How do you seek to honor God in the way you steward the resources He has given you?

notes

Week 2 Day 1: The Point of No Return — 63

We are to look to Christ, who was perfectly just
and righteous on our behalf.

Week 2 Day 2

Seek the Lord and Live

> Practice This Week's Memory Verse

> Read Amos 5:1–17

The last of Amos's announcement oracles is written using a chiastic structure, meaning that themes are presented and then repeated in reverse order. This is a literary device often used in the Bible to explain and emphasize the author's main point. Review each section as you read to get a feel for the structure Amos uses for his oracle. After you review, we will work through each theme one by one.

```
A    A Lament Over Israel's Demise (5:1–3)
 B   A Call To Seek The Lord (5:4–6)
  C  Rejecting The Call (5:7)
   D Doxology (5:8–9)
  C' Rejecting The Call (5:10–13)
 B'  A Call To Seek The Lord (5:14–15)
A'   A Lament Over Israel's Demise (5:16–17)
```

A Lament over Israel's Demise
Review Amos 5:1–3, 16–17

A rich doxology of God's power over all creation (Amos 4:13) now gives way to a sorrowful lament. While the Israelites have been enjoying their extravagant lifestyles, they do so without realizing that their days are numbered. In Hebrew, "lament" can also mean "elegy" or "dirge," so for Amos to sing a lament means it's as if he is mourning a death. In other words, Israel is hearing their own eulogy as Amos describes the fall of their nation. The first three verses in this section offer a crushing representation of Israel's condition.

After neglecting each opportunity to turn back to the Lord (Amos 4:6–11), Israel is now alone with no one there to help. The army meant to protect her will be defeated. When the theme of lament is repeated in verses 16 and 17, we learn that wailing and mourning in areas of public life will be all that remains among the ashes. Echoing the language of the Passover in Exodus 12:12, God will pass among His people. However, unlike the Passover, God's judgment upon Israel is all but certain.

A Call to Seek the Lord
Review Amos 5:4–6, 14–15

The lament shifts from death to life as Amos pleads with the Israelites to "seek the Lord and live" (Amos 5:6). Amos warns against going to the places Israel frequently worshiped, as he ironically mentioned in Amos 4:4. These places were originally monuments to remember the Lord's faithfulness but, over the generations, had become shrines of false worship. Going to these shrines to seek God would actually further condemn them. Not only that, but God will destroy them also as He sends them into exile. Fire is once again used as God's means of judgment as Amos describes how He will destroy the house of Joseph. Israel is as good as dead (Amos 5:2), yet God has still made a way for the righteous to seek Him and find life. If Israel turns from evil and pursues the things of God, God promises to be with His people (Amos 5:14) and be gracious to the faithful remnant (Amos 5:15). Seeking the Lord means devoting yourself to the causes to which He is devoted.

Rejecting the Call
Review Amos 5:7, 10–13

Israel has failed to model their lives after the God of justice and righteousness (Psalm 89:14). Justice is the act of fair sentencing and sound judgment, while righteousness is upright conduct and holy living before God. To live a life that stands for justice and righteousness is to worship God as He is perfectly just and righteous. But instead, Amos says Israel treats justice like wormwood, a poisonous

plant. Justice goes untouched, lest it causes a reaction, and righteousness is thrown on the ground, trampled on, and neglected. Israel hates fair judges and despises credible witnesses. Oppression is so prevalent in their land that others remain silent, unable to stand up for what is right without risking their lives. As a result, they will be unable to enjoy the fruits of their oppressive labor.

Doxology
Review Amos 5:8–9

Amos inserts a doxology as the centerpiece of this chiasm. As we discussed yesterday, a doxology expresses praise to God, and with this doxology, Amos reminds Israel of the very nature of the God they have chosen to reject. God's power is over the sun and the stars, the false gods that other religions worship. His sovereign hand decides when dawn breaks each morning and when darkness falls on the earth. He can bring drought, and He can bring floods. He can bring devastation, and He can bring restoration. This unlimited and all-powerful God stands in contrast to those who seek to wield power for their own benefit.

Israel's life did not promote justice and righteousness. Jesus fought the Pharisees in His day to see justice enacted as He condemned them for the same reasons—neglecting the Law and the good of others in favor of hypocritical religious behavior. This was highlighted when Jesus said, "Woe to you, scribes and Pharisees, hypocrites! You pay a tenth of mint, dill, and cumin, and yet you have neglected the more important matters of the law—justice, mercy, and faithfulness. These things should have been done without neglecting the others. Blind guides! You strain out a gnat, but gulp down a camel!" (Matthew 23:23–24).

The world is still full of injustice. We see it in our communities, in our own lives, and in the lives of those closest to us. What are we called to do when faced with such injustice? We are to look to Christ, who was perfectly just and righteous on our behalf. Additionally, we are to look like Christ, pursuing good and hating evil. Fixing our eyes on Christ will help us seek the things He cares about most—loving God and loving His people.

reflect

After studying this chiasm, what is the main idea that Amos is communicating? How does this chiastic structure emphasize his point?

In what ways is God just and righteous? How should the life of a Christian reflect these aspects of His character?

Summarize each of the three announcement oracles covered in the book of Amos. What was the emphasis of each one? What similarities or differences do you see between them?

Review: Amos's Three Announcement Oracles *(Amos 3:1–5:17)*		
1. Amos 3:1–15	*2. Amos 4:1–13*	*3. Amos 5:1–17*

Similarities in the Oracles:

Differences between the Oracles:

notes

If you trust in the work of Christ for your salvation, you do not have to fear.

Week 2 Day 3

From Exodus to Exile

> Practice This Week's Memory Verse

> Read Amos 5:18–27, Psalm 51

The sorrowful tone continues as Amos proclaims his first woe oracle against the religious hypocrites. Israel longed for "the day of the Lord," a time when they expected their enemies to be defeated. But in Amos 5:18–20, Amos subverts the Israelites' expectations for that day. They saw the day of the Lord as the day of victory and redemption, but like many of the other prophets who would come after him, Amos makes it clear that it will be a day of judgment. As we will see in chapter 7, Amos desires mercy for God's people (Amos 7:2). He seems to take no pleasure in warning them to see this day for what it truly is.

The theme of darkness and light is woven throughout the book of Amos. In this passage, the darkness emphasizes that the day of the Lord is not a day the Israelites should be anticipating. It is a day of reckoning that they should fear in light of their wickedness. They cling to a false sense of security as God's chosen people, but punishment for their sin will be swift and severe. With each oracle and proclamation, it seems that everything Israel had come to expect as God's elect is being turned upside down.

Amos boldly expresses how God views their pagan-influenced worship by telling Israel how He hates and despises their acts of worship. This type of language is often used in Scripture when referencing one's enemies, once again adjusting Israel's expectations from anticipation to fear. The stench of their hypocrisy is so horrible that God refuses to endure it any longer. God had provided ways for His people to fellowship with Him, but the Israelites distorted and perverted these means of grace.

God's displeasure with empty sacrifices is well documented throughout the Bible. In Psalm 51:17, David cries out to the Lord as he confesses and repents of his sin against a holy God: "The sacrifice pleasing to God is a broken spirit. You will not despise a broken and humbled heart, God." Contrast David's posture with the posture of the Israelites in the book of Amos, and it is clear they are neither broken nor humble in heart over their sin.

God breaks through this dark and gloomy oracle to reveal what really pleases Him: "But let justice flow like water, and righteousness, like an unfailing stream" (Amos 5:24). This is the cry of the downtrodden and oppressed. Justice and righteousness are at the very heart of God. This right way of living should flow from Israel's covenantal relationship with God. Instead, the Israelites tried to feign obedience in certain areas, like public offerings and sacrifices, while neglecting much of what the Law requires. The desire for unhindered justice and ever-flowing righteousness should fill our hearts and transform how we treat God's image-bearers.

God rejects half-hearted obedience and empty offerings of worship, and Amos presents a stark contrast to Israel's way of life in Amos 5:24. It is a call to action, even for us today. This is what a life of following and worshiping God should look like. God calls us to be fully devoted to Him while living our lives as an overflow of His great love toward us.

The God of the Exodus, who led Israel out of bondage and into freedom, is now sending His people into exile. This should be very telling for us as readers as it suggests that Israel did not heed God's call to "seek me and live" (Amos 5:4). Instead, they sought their own pleasures and faced the judgment they were

warned about. Throughout Israel's history, the Word of God had been distorted and diminished. They worshiped pagan gods alongside God in the sanctuaries, equating the one true God to false gods that humans made. Like Adam and Eve in the garden, they rejected the way of the Lord in favor of their own way of living (2 Kings 17:14–15).

The day of the Lord brings redemption to some and rejection to others. We were once like the Israelites, pursuing our own pleasures and comfort. But if we are in Christ, we do not have to wonder what this day will be like for us. It will be a day to look forward to when all things are made right. Still, it can be difficult for us to fully comprehend what that day will be like. For some of us, we may worry if we are truly saved. In one of his New Testament letters, the Apostle Paul encouraged the church at Thessalonica, which was wrestling with many of the same things. Paul reminded them, "For you are all children of light and children of the day. We do not belong to the night or the darkness" (1 Thessalonians 5:5). If you trust in the work of Christ for your salvation, you do not have to fear. For the believer, the day of the Lord will not be a day of darkness and gloom but of light and hope. We live our entire lives in view of this day, living as exiles until Christ returns to consummate an even greater exodus and brings us home. Because of the shed blood of Christ, we are now children of light, and we get to enjoy God's glorious presence for all eternity.

> Because of the shed blood of Christ, we are now children of light.

reflect

Look for each reference to darkness in the book of Amos.
(Use a website like blueletterbible.org if you get stuck.)
What differences do you see in the way Amos uses
the theme of darkness throughout the book?

How does Psalm 51 reveal what God loves? How does it
impact the way you understand this passage in Amos?

What are some practical ways you can pursue justice
and righteousness in how you treat others?

notes

In God's kindness, the Holy Spirit reveals
the false securities we cling to in our own lives.

Week 2 Day 4

Pride Comes Before the Fall

Practice This Week's Memory Verse

Read Amos 6:1–14

With each pronouncement of God's judgment, Amos peels back another layer of outward religiosity to reveal the Israelites' false sense of security under the surface. Amos's second woe oracle calls out the overindulgent and seemingly self-sufficient practices that marked Israel's society. It is as if Amos is pulling back pristine carpeting to expose weakened, rotten floorboards underneath, ready to give way at any moment. The foundation of their entire way of living is crumbling.

Amos opens this oracle in an unexpected way by referring to those who are at ease in Zion. Zion is mentioned only one other time when the book opens with the Lord roaring from Zion (Amos 1:2). Amos levels the playing field by addressing Zion—which refers to Jerusalem, the capital of Judah—and Samaria, the capital of Israel, in the same way. In doing so, Amos reminds each nation that they are no better than the other. While they may be confident in the strength of their cities, Amos points to other cities that have already fallen—Calneh, Hamath, and Gath—as a warning that they are not exempt from a similar fate.

Israel had a distorted view of their covenant relationship with God. They saw the covenant as a "one and done" sort of agreement that gave them the license to live however they wanted. Like a petulant child, the Israelites did not seem to give a second thought to how their behavior impacted others, turning a blind eye to the consequences of their actions. They neglected justice in favor of pursuing wealth and taking bribes while overlooking the needs of the poor and marginalized (Amos 5:10–13).

Israel's interactions with God and other people were merely transactional, not relational. God's people refused to see their need for repentance; thus, their pride led them into exile. Just as they were first in society, God chose the influential and prominent figures to be first to go into captivity. All of the comforts Israel had come to expect in life would come crashing down (Amos 6:7).

The Lord God swears by Himself once again as He denounces Israel's pride in created things, such as the strength of their citadels and their military expertise. In verses 8–14, God describes the utter devastation this exile would bring upon His people. While the details of the story Amos tells in verses 9 and 10 may be unclear, the intended message is evident. There will be such dread that the people would not even say the name of the Lord God for fear of incurring more of His wrath.

In Amos 6:12, there is a callback to Amos 5:7 with the repeated motif of justice and righteousness being turned into poison. Amos points out the absurdity of Israel boasting in their own military strength when God's power will wipe out any semblance of stability. And as Amos concludes this oracle, he reveals that God will raise up *another* nation, an enemy of His chosen people, to carry out God's judgment against them. This conquest would not impact just a few cities. It would be widespread over the entire nation "from the entrance of Hamath to the Brook of the Arabah" (verse 14). If Israel was still unsure of the extent of this punishment at this point, this oracle probably provided some clarity. God's wrath was indeed coming for His people.

God exposed Israel's hearts by addressing their worship of comfort displayed through their complacency and apathy toward Him and others. This points to the fallen condition of humanity. In our flesh, we do not grieve over sin. We look to our own interests over the needs of others. We accumulate wealth and power in hopes of being recognized as notable and important. Like the Israelites, we can attempt to have a relationship with God on our own terms, looking for how it might benefit us.

In God's kindness, the Holy Spirit reveals the false securities we cling to in our own lives. Our self-sufficiency is evident when we see dependence on the Lord as a weakness rather than a strength. The idol of comfort—our complacency and love of pleasure—is exposed when we seek a pain-free life instead of laying down our lives and taking up our cross to follow Jesus. Only when we rely upon God for our security do we see the sufficiency of the gospel for all of life. Looking to Christ's finished work on the cross can soften even the hardest of hearts, and it brings us to our knees in humble adoration of the King of kings.

> Looking to Christ's finished work on the cross can soften even the hardest of hearts.

reflect

When do you look to your own strength instead of relying on God?

Do you seek to have a posture of repentance? What does it look like to grieve your sin and turn toward Him in obedience?

In what ways have you grown complacent in your relationship with the Lord?

notes

God has provided us with
all we need to live godly lives

Week 2 Day 5

The Unrelenting Lord

Practice This Week's Memory Verse

Read Amos 7:1–17

The prophets are known for their use of vivid imagery, and as we have seen thus far, Amos is no exception. Amos has employed some memorable imagery throughout this book, from the Lord roaring like a lion to comparing righteous living to rushing water. This chapter shows a shift in how Amos's message is communicated. God gives Amos not only words to speak but captivating visuals to describe to His people. With each vision, Amos continues to emphasize that these visions come from the Lord (verses 1, 4, and 7).

God shows Amos locusts and fire in his first two visions, which are commonly used to represent God's judgment throughout the Old Testament (Exodus 10:12, Deuteronomy 28:38, Joel 1:4, Isaiah 66:16, Ezekiel 28:18). The locusts in the first vision destroy Israel's crops, which would devastate their food supply for the year. In the second vision, fire destroys everything in its path. And in both visions, Amos pleads for God's mercy on behalf of Israel, and the Lord relents, deciding against the intended punishment.

This may cause some confusion, especially as we look to a third vision where God does not relent. Does this mean God changed His mind? Can humans dictate the actions of God? Why does He relent in some situations but not others? When we are unsure how to interpret verses like these, it is important to keep in mind the totality of God's Word. We want Scripture to interpret Scripture, meaning we should see what all of the Bible has to say about any particular topic rather than reading a verse or two out of context.

Throughout the Old Testament, we see instances of God relenting from punishment. In Exodus 32, God relents because of Moses's appeal to God's covenantal faithfulness as he intercedes on behalf of the Israelites. In some situations, we see that God relents because of people's changed hearts. An example of this is from Jonah 3:10, which reads, "God saw their actions—that they had turned from their evil ways—so God relented from the disaster he had threatened them with. And he did not do it." This is what Amos is hoping to see in the Israelites—softened hearts that desire God and turn from their evil ways. God chooses to be patient and relent, but His patience will run out eventually, as we see in the third vision.

In this vision, Amos sees God standing next to a vertical wall with a plumb line, which is a weight tied to a string that determines if a wall is straight. While most modern Bibles translate the Hebrew word *ănāk* as "plumb line," the origin of this word is a mystery to many scholars. Some translations use it to mean "plaster," "tin," or "something that is narrow." If it is understood to be something similar to tin, it could refer to a wall that looks straight and solid but, in reality, is a weak facade made to look strong. Whether you interpret *ănāk* as "tin" or "a plumb line," God is showing that Israel has gone so far off track that their desires and behaviors are no longer aligned with His holy standard.

Amos has a very different response in the third vision than the previous ones. Unlike Jonah, who opposed giving the Ninevites another chance, Amos pleads with the Lord to extend His grace. However, by the third vision, Amos understands. All hope is lost for the nation of Israel, whose hearts are enamored by worldly pleasures. God promises that He will inflict this punishment against the house of Jeroboam, informing them that their time is up. The Lord's patience is gone, and He will no longer spare them.

Amaziah is the priest in Bethel's sanctuary and is closely connected with the king of Israel, Jeroboam II. When he hears about this doomsday street preacher named Amos threatening to dismantle their way of living, Amaziah tries to expel him from their city. This narrative break in the list of visions may seem a bit out of place, but consider the vision that precedes this story. Amaziah's opposition to Amos and his message illustrates how far Israel had strayed. Amaziah was unwilling to hear the voice of God through His servant Amos, and in trying to silence Amos, the priest was trying to silence the message of God. The inclusion of this story affirms Amos's identity as someone chosen and called by God to prophesy to Israel. It also gives us some indication that Amos faced opposition as he preached God's message.

It can be tempting to look at Amos's story and think: *Of course Amos was obedient. God revealed Himself and spoke to him in visions. If only I saw visions and heard the voice of God!* But reflect on the disciples' journey in the Gospel accounts. They had their Messiah in the flesh, yet they faltered and even rejected Him at times. The problem does not lie with how God chooses to reveal Himself—the problem lies in our desire to pursue worldly wisdom and fulfillment apart from God.

God has provided us with all we need to live godly lives (2 Peter 1:3). For Israel, He provided the Law and prophets like Amos who communicated God's message. For us today, God has given us His Word and His Spirit who dwells within us. Even when we falter, God is faithful to draw near to us. God is patient and merciful, but He also demands that we are holy because He is holy (1 Peter 1:16). Just like Israel, we have been given God's message through His Word. The more we read it and treasure it, the more we will look like Him in our pursuit of holiness.

reflect

How does 2 Peter 1:3 encourage you in your pursuit of holiness?

How does Amos's response to the Lord in the visions reveal his heart toward those he is ministering to? How does this challenge you as you share the gospel with those around you?

Amos was obedient to God's call on his life, even when he met opposition. What opposition do you face? How can you set aside the things that hinder you as you seek obedience (Hebrews 12:1)?

notes

Week 3 Introduction

Hope for a Future

As we close our study in Amos, we will see the proverbial light at the end of the tunnel. However, for Israel, it will get worse before it gets better. Israel has continually rejected God as their king. They disobeyed His commands and turned to worldly pleasures. They abused their power to oppress others and delighted in their wealth rather than delighting in the one true God. God's patience has run out for Israel.

In the final verses of the book, God's faithfulness shines bright in the darkness as Israel is promised ultimate restoration. If you feel like there are people or situations in your life that are beyond repair, the conclusion of Amos should bring you hope. Nothing is beyond the reach of Christ's redemptive love.

Before you begin this third week of study content, spend time reviewing the previous week's chapters and memory verse. Pray that the Lord would help you to delight in Him as you study His Word. Ask God to protect your heart against lesser loves competing for your affections. Use the space below to write out a simple prayer before starting week three's content.

Memory Verse

If we are faithless, he remains faithful,
for he cannot deny himself.

2 Timothy 2:13

The fruit of obedience flourishes
in the soil of a dependent heart.

Week 3 Day 1

Feast to Famine

> Practice This Week's Memory Verse

> Read Amos 8:1–14

In the eighth century BC, the economic gap widened between the richest and the poorest classes in Israel's society. The wealthy Israelites found ways to exploit the marginalized while adhering to an adapted version of modern religion. This included syncretistic worship, which, as a reminder, means the people worshiped gods from the different religions of their day alongside the God of Israel, the true God. God abhors such conduct and cannot allow for this to continue under the pretense of true faith. The Israelites' man-made religion that brought them to this point cannot save them now.

This chapter opens with another vision—this time, with a fruit basket, which seems unusual as a symbol of God's judgment. The imagery becomes clearer as we understand how Amos has utilized language to emphasize his point. Amos is employing some wordplay that sometimes gets lost in modern-day translations. The Hebrew word for summer fruit is *qayiṣ*, which sounds a lot like the Hebrew word *qēṣ*, meaning "end." Reading passages in a few other translations can help one understand passages like these. The New Living Translation incorporates the double meaning of the words into its translation: "'What do you see, Amos?' he asked. I replied, 'A basket full of ripe fruit.' Then the Lord said, 'Like this fruit, Israel is ripe for punishment! I will not delay their punishment again'" (Amos 8:2 NLT).

God will no longer wait—the end has come for Israel. The opportunity to repent from their sin is gone. Amos's message of judgment has been stripped of its silver lining—no more calls to seek the Lord and live (Amos 5:4). It is time for Israel to come to grips with the harsh reality they will face in the coming years. Their season of abundance will soon give way to a season of emptiness.

Following this vision, Amos presents more evidence for judgment against Israel, as well as God's response to Israel. The accusation is centered around, yet again, trampling on the needy and mistreating the poor. In Amos 2:6–7, Amos called out the various ways that religious hypocrisy permeated Israelite society. Now, he is continuing to condemn the horrific treatment of people through slavery. Merchants cheated the poor by overcharging them, then they turned around and used that profit to purchase the poor as slaves. It became a cruel cycle of poverty perpetuated by the hands of God's people.

The Israelites adhered to the Jewish traditions, such as the Sabbath and the New Moon festival, meant to remind them of God's faithfulness (Numbers 10:10). But Amos 8:5 reveals their hearts: "When will the New Moon be over so we may sell grain, and the Sabbath, so we can market wheat?" Their motives rise to the surface: "We can reduce the measure while increasing the price and cheat with dishonest scales." These are not the words of pagans but supposed God-fearing Israelites. They knew God and His commands, yet they completely disregarded biblical worship and ethics.

Amos has laid out the evidence against Israel—impure worship, motives, and behavior—so now he details their just punishment. God swears an oath that He will never forget the actions of His people and reveals what Israel will experience. Many scholars believe Amos is referring to an earthquake (Amos 8:8) and an eclipse (Amos 8:9). We know that an earthquake occurs within two years of Amos's prophecy (Amos 1:1), so this may be the event that verse 8 describes.

God's authority and power are made evident: "I will make . . . I will darken . . ." (verse 9), "I will turn . . . I will cause . . . I will make . . ." (verse 10), "I will send . . ." (verse 11). These things Israel will soon endure will not just happen by chance. The wrath poured out from God's sovereign hand is upon them.

In all of their adherence to religious festivals and ceremonies, Israel has neglected the ultimate purpose of it—God Himself. They have taken for granted their access to God's Word, and now God is removing it (verse 11). When they experience suffering and look to God for comfort, they will not find it. When they search far and wide, they will come up empty. They will not hear a word from the Lord. There will only be wailing, for the end has come. The fruit has rotted and withered away.

Fruit grows in healthy soil that is cultivated and nourished, and the same can be said for our own lives. The question is, what kind of fruit are we producing? Is it the fruit of self-reliance that will rot and be thrown away? Israel bore this kind of fruit, and it led to their destruction. Jesus says in John 15:5 that the only way we can provide any kind of good fruit is to remain in Him alone. The fruit of obedience flourishes in the soil of a dependent heart.

Amos has shown us that we will become what we worship. Israel's focus had turned away from the one true God and toward maintaining a cultural, surface-level religion that cultivated a worship of self. Israel became self-focused rather than God-focused. They were meant to be a beacon of hope to those who did not know the Lord. God's people were to enact His goodness in the way they cared for others. Though His people were hard-hearted, unable to keep His commands, God had not forgotten His promises. He would remain faithful.

Like Israel, we are just as deserving of punishment for our sin. We can easily turn to man-made things to give us purpose and satisfaction, worshiping the created rather than the Creator. We are unable to stand before God without a meditator. Jesus fully paid the penalty for our sins through His shed blood on the cross. Now we have access to God through Christ, our perfect mediator (1 Timothy 2:5–6). When we behold our ever-faithful God and worship Him in spirit and truth, we will become more like Him, reflecting His glory and living out an authentic faith.

reflect

Read Galatians 5:16–25. What evidence of the Spirit do you see in your life? In what areas would you like to grow?

What overall themes from the book does Amos draw out in chapter 8? Search for words or phrases that have been repeated in past chapters and look for the significance of these words or phrases in the book.

Theme	Verse(s)	Significance

Examine your own spiritual life. Are there ways you have adopted a "cultural" form of Christianity?

notes

God sees all, knows all, and can do all.
Nothing is outside of God's control.

Week 3 Day 2

The All-Knowing God of Armies

> Practice This Week's Memory Verse

> Read Amos 9:1–6, Hebrews 10:26–31

Just when we think the darkness cannot get any worse for Israel, they are plunged further into the depths of despair. Amos describes one last vision where the Lord calls for the destruction of all they have ever known. Their place of worship will become a house of despair as it crashes onto them with nowhere to hide. Imagine being in Amos's shoes, preaching this message to a seemingly doomed audience. He is like a doctor who tells a patient that they are in the final stages of a terminal illness and then goes into detail about how they will suffer in their last days.

It is a bleak picture that Amos is painting for us, but at this point in our study, we should not be surprised. The call for obedience has gone unanswered. The plea for the Lord's mercy has been rejected. God established His covenant with Israel long ago, along with blessings for obedience and curses for disobedience (Deuteronomy 28). With that in mind, this should not be surprising for Israel either. They will reap what they have sown.

The entire book of Amos illustrates how Israel relegated God to being a background character in their everyday lives. In this chapter, the King takes His rightful place, center stage, declaring His glorious power. No matter where they go or what they do, they will never be out of God's sight. Amos describes how God will reach them no matter where they try to escape: in the depths of Sheol or the highest point in heaven, on the top of Mount Carmel or at the very bottom of the seafloor. Even exile will not end their suffering as they will continue to experience His wrath.

The emphasis in this opening section is God's omnipresence and omnipotence (verses 1–4). God sees all, knows all, and can do all. Nothing is outside of God's control. It all passes through the sovereign hands of the creator God. He concludes this section with the chilling statement in verse 4, "I will keep my eye on them for harm and not for good."

The next section, Amos 9:5–6, contains the last of the three doxologies found in the book of Amos (Amos 4:13, 5:8–9). Amos continues to emphasize God's sovereignty over all of creation, even the places of escape (9:2–3). As we are coming to the end of the book, it is clear why these doxologies are included. Amos was sent to preach this message because Israel had forgotten their first love. They had allowed the gods of money, comfort, and power to reside in their hearts. These doxologies act as their teacher, to instruct them in the great power of *Yahweh*, the God of Armies.

How do we reconcile the darkness in Israel's history with the beauty of God's grace? The God who promised never to forsake His people has also told them that His eye is on them for harm and not for good. Both of these can be held in perfect tension in the hands of a faithful, unchanging God. Moses was clear that anyone who did not obey the commands of God would be subject to devastating consequences (Deuteronomy 28:15). God is not a parent who threatens to discipline a child but fails to follow through. That would contradict His very nature. Israel's unfaithfulness must be punished.

We might read passages like this and file them away under the category of "The God of the Old Testament." In doing so, we try to make sense of difficult truths by dismissing what seems impractical or irreconcilable. But the God of the Old Testament is the God of the New Testament. The things He cares about, acts on, and pursues are the same throughout all of history. In Exodus 34:6–7, God describes His nature to Moses as compassionate and slow to anger—yet He will not leave the guilty unpunished. We experience tension as we seek to understand God's character. He extends grace but also punishment. It may feel as if some of God's attributes fight against each other, but in reality, they are all enveloped within God's perfect nature. We see this displayed in the gospel as both justice and grace are fully realized at the cross. If we are in Christ, the price for our sin has already been paid. The judgment that we deserve for our sin falls on Christ. We are credited with His righteousness as if we lived His perfect life. What a glorious reality we often neglect to consider!

This is a sobering text that reveals the depth of Israel's punishment and the grandeur of our creator God. As you reflect on this passage, and Amos as a book, think about your own faith journey. Even if you come from a Christian home or you attend church every week, we can all be deceived into thinking that our standing before God is secure apart from the finished work of Christ. In doing so, we follow the pattern of the Israelites, presuming upon God's kindness and grace because of our heritage, upbringing, or good works. And just like the Israelites, we are deserving of judgment when we worship ourselves over Christ. If we are in Christ—meaning that we have placed our faith in God alone for our salvation and trust in Jesus's atoning death to cover our sins—the judgment falls on Christ instead of us.

If the book of Amos ended here, there would be no hope of a future for God's people. However, as you will see over the next few days, this final chapter that begins with destruction concludes with hope for a future. Even if we struggle to know what to do with a passage like this, we trust that these words are God's words, inspired and profitable (2 Timothy 3:16). Let us rejoice that God gave us access to Himself and His Word, including the message of His servant Amos.

reflect

What comes to mind when you think about God's sovereignty?

How has God become a background character in your life?
What would it look like for God to be at the center of all you do?

Review all of the doxologies in Amos (Amos 4:13, 5:8–9, and 9:5–6).
What is emphasized about God's character in all three of these passages?

God's hand is still upon His people,
and His plan of redemption
remains unhindered.

Week 3 Day 3

Sifting of the Nations

> Practice This Week's Memory Verse

> Read Amos 9:7–10

A sliver of light breaks through the vast darkness. The promise of deliverance illuminates the continued faithfulness of God in the midst of Israel's unfaithfulness. God's hand is still upon His people, and His plan of redemption remains unhindered.

The underlying theme throughout Amos is the security the Israelites found in their national identity and societal status. So when they heard God comparing them to the Cushites, a foreign and far-away people group who lived south of Egypt, they were probably confused or even offended. God chose Israel to be set apart, a people for His own possession (Deuteronomy 7:6, 14:2). Why would God put them in the same category as some other people group? God then takes it a step further by comparing their exodus out of Egypt to that of their pagan neighbors. If they were not confused or offended by the first comparison, surely they were now. God is putting the most significant event in Israel's history alongside their enemies. God sovereignly orchestrated moving these different groups to their homeland, just as He did for His own people, displaying how Israel is just like her Gentile neighbors in many ways.

The sin of Israel brought darkness into their world and invited God's wrath to fall upon them. Yes, God would also bring punishment on other nations, as we saw in chapter 1. Yet Israel, too, had now become a "sinful kingdom" (verse 8). They assumed that because they had experienced God's blessing and protection in the past, they could continue to expect those things in the future. But while God had promised in His covenant with Israel to bless them if they were obedient, He also promised to judge them if they disobeyed Him (Deuteronomy 28). And now, in His covenant faithfulness, He would act accordingly. Amos has emphasized this from the very beginning as he laid out the crimes of the nations, which included Judah and Israel. Far from shielding them from judgment, their status as God's elect gave them increased responsibilities to obey Him, not less.

However, God's holiness is beautifully intertwined with His faithfulness as He promises not to destroy Israel completely. God had already pointed to their redemption when He compared it to snatching a wounded animal from the mouth of a lion (Amos 3:12). Amos also uses the imagery of a sieve, which was a tool used to filter out foreign objects or impurities like chaff from the rest of the grain. The pebbles (verse 9) or "sinners" (verse 10) are the Israelites who still attempt to rely upon their national identity for protection, claiming the name of Israelite while living the life of a pagan. They will be identified as impure and sifted out. Just as God is powerful enough to destroy the wicked, He is also just as powerful to sift through the wreckage to save His people.

In verse 8, God says, "I will not totally destroy the house of Jacob." The promise that God would not completely destroy Israel affirms His promise to Abraham made long ago to multiply his descendants and bless all nations through them (Genesis 12:1–3). These words of deliverance bring hope to a future beyond exile and destruction. This is not the end of Israel's story. And it is not the end of ours.

When our world was full of darkness, the Son of God broke through as the dawning of a new day. He entered into our brokenness and shame and established a new covenant—one based on grace for those who believe in Him. The true purpose of His promise is coming to bring more light into the dark world. Because of the new covenant, when God looks at us, He does not see sin to judge, mistakes to condemn, or wickedness to punish. He sees the perfect righteousness of His Son. We are clothed in His righteousness, and this informs our identity—not our past good works or our future sins.

The same watchful gaze of the Lord is upon us today. And just like Israel, our current relationship with the Lord is what determines our future. Take some time to reflect on what defines your faith. Our salvation is not determined by our religious upbringing or how many times we read our Bible and attend church. It lies within the gospel that is "the power of God for salvation to everyone who believes, first to the Jew, and also to the Greek" (Romans 1:16). Our good works are not what save us. Instead, our good works flow from faith in God alone for our salvation.

> When our world was full of darkness, the Son of God broke through as the dawning of a new day.

reflect

What other identities are you tempted to rest
in apart from your identity in Christ?

Reflect on all that you have been given as a child of God.
How can operating from this identity change
your priorities and perspectives?

Israel relied on the past to give them security and comfort for the
future. In what ways do you rely on your past religious experiences or
events for comfort rather than looking to the finished work of Christ?

notes

God is in the business of breathing purpose
into what is broken.

Week 3 Day 4

Hope is Here

> Practice This Week's Memory Verse

> Read Amos 9:11–12, 2 Samuel 7:1–16

Every word of this book, each oracle and vision, has been leading up to this. At last, there is true hope for the faithful remnant, sifted from the wreckage, who obey the call to seek the Lord and live (Amos 5:4). It may feel a bit jarring moving from the death of those in denial of God's judgment in verse 10 to the promise of restoration in verse 11. The extreme shift in tone has caused some scholars to debate if this portion was original to Amos's message or added at a later time by an editor of the book.

However, though the tone changes dramatically in these closing verses, it is still consistent with Amos's message. There is salvation to be found for those who seek the Lord and reject the cultural religion of their day. This does not negate the judgment leveled against Israel, but it takes into account those who truly worshiped *Yahweh* and lived a life that reflected Him. They would not be forgotten amidst the destruction of the wicked.

This is the first of two salvation oracles that conclude the book of Amos. The day of the Lord comes into view again as God provides hope for those who earnestly seek Him. The Lord speaks of this day, not in terms of judgment and darkness but glorious hope. Though chapter 9 opens with destruction, it closes with restoration. God promises to restore the "fallen shelter of David" (verse 11). No other details are given about how the Davidic kingdom will be restored, just that it will happen and that God will be the One to do it.

Over a century prior to Amos, a different Jeroboam was king. During the split of the northern and southern kingdoms, Jeroboam I ruled over Israel in the north. In 1 Kings 12, Jeroboam I rejected Rehoboam—David's grandson and Solomon's son, who was to be the next king—and thus rejected Davidic rule. As time went on, kings in both kingdoms served their own wants and needs rather than serving God and His people. So, by the time of Amos's message, the Davidic monarchy was in shambles. Yet here we find hope for Israel's future in the promised restoration of the Davidic kingdom. A king from the house of David would rule once again.

In addition to the restoration of the house of David, there is also an inclusion of a remnant of Edom. The Edomites were Israel's enemies and persecutors, and they were mentioned several times in the first two chapters of Amos. They were just as guilty in their sin, yet they would also be redeemed and included in the people of God. This would accomplish God's plan that all the nations, not just Israel, would worship Him as Lord.

In Acts 15:13–17, James quotes this passage from Amos during the Jerusalem Council to prove that the inclusion of Gentiles within the church had always been God's plan. God's plan of redemption has always looked to a day when all people would be blessed and come to know Him, as evidenced in the Abrahamic covenant (Genesis 12:1–3). The Apostle Paul also heavily emphasized the relationship between Jews and Gentiles in his writings. In his letter to the Ephesian church, Paul writes, "The Gentiles are coheirs, members of the same body, and partners in the promise in Christ Jesus through the gospel" (Ephesians 3:6). There is no distinction based on heritage, for our identity is rooted in the gospel alone.

The purpose of God's judgment was not for the complete destruction of His people but for restoration. Destruction is not the end of Israel's story—hope has come. Reflect on the words used to describe this hope—"restore," "repair," "rebuild." God is in the business of breathing purpose into what is broken. Those words hold such hopeful expectation, but their weight and trustworthiness are held ultimately in God Himself as He promises to be the One to accomplish this for His people. God's restoration is not dependent on anyone but Himself. Amos has revealed the hearts of the Israelites, exposing all their selfish motivations and sinful behavior. Now the focus is on the heart of God and how He continually displays His faithfulness. Just as God made a covenant with Abraham, He made a covenant with David that from his family, God would raise up a descendant to establish a kingdom that would last forever (2 Samuel 7:12–13, 16).

As Israel split into two kingdoms and as God's people turned away from Him, the fulfillment of His promises seemed to be out of reach. Even still, God remained faithful throughout the years. That promised descendant came many years later, born of a virgin in the town of Bethlehem. That baby would be the "Son of David, the Son of Abraham" (Matthew 1:1), whose kingdom would last forever and whose reign would have no end. Restoration is only made possible through the life, death, and resurrection of Jesus, the true and better David.

There are things in life that feel like they are beyond repair and without hope. We experience the brokenness of our world as we face fractured relationships, physical ailments, and the loss of loved ones. The promise of restoration lifts our gaze to the God who restores, repairs, and rebuilds. God always keeps His promises. He will always act on behalf of His people.

> The promise of restoration lifts our gaze to the God who restores, repairs, and rebuilds.

reflect

Why is it significant that Edom is included among those who would be redeemed? What impact does that have on the Church today?

What words would you use to describe your faith? How do these words reflect your current walk with the Lord?

What in your life seems beyond repair? How does this passage help you to trust the Lord with those situations?

God is continually at work,
making beauty out of ashes.

Week 3 Day 5

A Future Restored

Practice This Week's Memory Verse

Read Amos 9:13–15

The shepherd from Tekoa embarked on quite the journey as he stepped into the role of a prophet. Amos obeyed God's call by taking His message to the nations and condemning their crimes against humanity before focusing solely on the transgressions carried out by those who claimed to bear God's name. Amos preached God's judgment and punishment to His chosen people in both kingdoms, facing opposition as he sought to obey God's will. Amos desired mercy upon God's people but understood the extent of their habitual unfaithfulness.

It seemed that their story would end in darkness as Israel would be taken captive and led out of their land into exile, just as God warned the generations before them (Deuteronomy 28:63–65). But, in God's rich mercy and fierce commitment to remain faithful to His promises, their story would continue beyond exile.

The final verses of Amos provide our second salvation oracle. Yesterday, we saw the promised restoration of the nations through the line of David. In this final oracle, God promises to restore the land and people. This is not just a promise to provide the bare minimum to survive. This is a glimpse into the abundant life that comes from a good Father. Amos uses hyperbolic language to describe how the land will be so plentiful that the workers will overlap in their duties because they will not be able to keep up with planting and harvesting. Its abundance will spill over the landscape—a continual reminder of God's providential care and love.

The restoration of people stands in contrast to the judgment God laid upon the hypocrites in Israel earlier in Amos 5:11: "Therefore, because you trample on the poor and exact a grain tax from him . . . you will never drink the wine from the lush vineyards you have planted." For the faithful remnant, God will give them what they have lost through drought and famine. He promises that they will see the fruit of their labor as they rebuild once-destroyed cities and enjoy the food and drink they work to produce.

It seems as though Israel desired security and sought it in every place but God Himself. They desired military strength, fortified cities, and material wealth. But this final verse in Amos provides the security they longed for as God promises that they will never be uprooted again. Their kingdom will be restored, the nations will worship God, their provision will be abundant, and as a people, they will be secure. This is the future promised to those who belong to the Lord.

Israel longed for a day when the promised King would come to claim victory, but once again, their view of salvation was seen from a political and military perspective. They desired victory over their enemies, but Christ came to defeat sin and death, fulfilling this promise given to God's people for a secure future.

The book concludes in the same way it began. The Lord roaring from Zion completes His message with a final declaration: "The Lord your God has spoken" (Amos 9:15). This reminds us that God speaks to us today through His Word, just as He spoke to His people through His servant Amos. The question is—are we listening? Do we neglect to sit still before the Lord to hear and obey His voice? God speaks loudly and powerfully through the Scriptures, proclaiming the gospel of His only Son, Jesus, who made a way for us to be saved.

Your heavenly Father desires for you to live an abundant life that comes from knowing and loving Him. And yet, the things of this world entangle us and threaten to pull us back into darkness. We are tempted to think that God is withholding from us in times of suffering or that He is absent from us in times of loneliness. We walk through trials, unsure whether God will provide. The history of Israel reminds us of God's unfailing mercy in the face of injustice. God sees the pain of His people, and He does not passively sit by watching. God is continually at work, making beauty out of ashes. He intervenes in hardship, but He also allows pain. Sometimes we do not know why, but we know He works for the good of His Church and the glory of His mighty name. We look ahead to the day when He will return to make all things new, when justice and righteousness will flow forever.

We can see our own mistakes reflected in the people of Israel, seeking our own way over the Lord's. We can feel as if we have gone too far for God's mercy. The book of Amos exposes the severity of sin and idolatry, but it also serves as a reminder that God remains faithful even when we are faithless (2 Timothy 2:13). He would not abandon His people. Sadly, many of the Israelites still chose to live a life of wicked debauchery, rejecting the abundant life found in God. Israel sought their security in perishable things, but in Christ, our future is secure with an imperishable inheritance (1 Peter 1:4). We are never too far gone to experience God's redemptive love in our lives. All we have to do is turn to Him, trusting in Christ's finished work on the cross. He fully paid for our sins. If we place our faith in Christ alone for our salvation, the abundant life is ours now and forever.

The message of Amos is for us today. Seek the Lord and live. He is sovereign over all of creation and history, and He is sovereign over the details of your life as well. Worship Him as the one true God. Your future is secure in Christ. Set aside anything that hinders you, and pursue the Lord with your whole heart, for He is worthy.

reflect

What are some things that might hinder you from living the abundant life God provides?

Review your answers from the first day of the study. What has God taught you as you studied Amos?

If someone were to ask you why it is important to study the book of Amos, what would you say?

What Is *the* Gospel?

Thank you for reading and enjoying this study with us! We are abundantly grateful for the Word of God, the instruction we glean from it, and the ever-growing understanding it provides for us of God's character. We are also thankful that Scripture continually points to one thing in innumerable ways: the gospel.

We remember our brokenness when we read about the fall of Adam and Eve in the garden of Eden (Genesis 3), where sin entered into a perfect world and maimed it. We remember the necessity that something innocent must die to pay for our sin when we read about the atoning sacrifices in the Old Testament. We read that we have all sinned and fallen short of the glory of God (Romans 3:23) and that the penalty for our brokenness, the wages of our sin, is death (Romans 6:23). We all need grace and mercy, but most importantly, we all need a Savior.

We consider the goodness of God when we realize that He did not plan to leave us in this dire state. We see His promise to buy us back from the clutches of sin and death in Genesis 3:15. And we see that promise accomplished with Jesus Christ on the cross. Jesus Christ knew no sin yet became sin so that we might become righteous through His sacrifice (2 Corinthians 5:21). Jesus was tempted in every way that we are and lived sinlessly. He was reviled yet still yielded Himself for our sake, that we may have life abundant in Him. Jesus lived the perfect life that we could not live and died the death that we deserved.

The gospel is profound yet simple. There are many mysteries in it that we will never understand this side of heaven, but there is still overwhelming weight to its implications in this life. The gospel tells of our sinfulness and God's goodness and a gracious gift that compels a response. We are saved by grace through faith, which means that we rest with faith in the grace that Jesus Christ displayed on the cross (Ephesians 2:8–9). We cannot save ourselves from our brokenness or do any amount of good works to merit God's favor. Still, we can have faith that what Jesus accomplished in His death, burial, and resurrection was more than enough for our salvation and our eternal delight. When we accept God, we are commanded to die to ourselves and our sinful desires and live a life worthy of the calling we have received (Ephesians 4:1). The gospel compels us to be sanctified, and in so doing, we are conformed to the likeness of Christ Himself. This is hope. This is redemption. This is the gospel.

GENESIS 3:15

I will put hostility between you and the woman, and between your offspring and her offspring. He will strike your head, and you will strike his heel.

ROMANS 3:23

For all have sinned and fall short of the glory of God.

ROMANS 6:23

For the wages of sin is death, but the gift of God is eternal life in Christ Jesus our Lord.

2 CORINTHIANS 5:21

He made the one who did not know sin to be sin for us, so that in him we might become the righteousness of God.

EPHESIANS 2:8-9

For you are saved by grace through faith, and this is not from yourselves; it is God's gift—not from works, so that no one can boast.

EPHESIANS 4:1-3

Therefore I, the prisoner in the Lord, urge you to walk worthy of the calling you have received, with all humility and gentleness, with patience, bearing with one another in love, making every effort to keep the unity of the Spirit through the bond of peace.

This is a glimpse into the abundant life that comes from a good Father.

Week 3 Day 5

BIBLIOGRAPHY

Fee, Gordon D., and Douglas K. Stuart. "Amos." *How to Read the Bible Book by Book: A Guided Tour*. Grand Rapids, MI: Zondervan, 2014.

Fyall, Bob. *Teaching Amos: From Text to Message*. Tain, Scotland: Christian Focus Publications, 2012.

Motyer, J. A. *The Message of Amos: The Day of the Lion*. Downers Grove, IL: IVP Academic, 1974.

NIV Biblical Theology Study Bible: Follow God's Redemptive Plan as It Unfolds throughout Scripture. Grand Rapids, MI: Zondervan, 2018.

Smith, Gary V. *The NIV Application Commentary: Hosea, Amos, Micah*. Grand Rapids, MI: Zondervan, 2001.

Stuart, Douglas. *Word Biblical Commentary: Hosea–Jonah*. Grand Rapids, MI: Zondervan, 1988.

Thank you for studying God's Word with us!

CONNECT WITH US

@thedailygraceco
@dailygracepodcast

CONTACT US

info@thedailygraceco.com

SHARE

#thedailygraceco

VISIT US ONLINE

www.thedailygraceco.com

MORE DAILY GRACE

Daily Grace® Podcast